The Truth Is

Poems by

Vivienne Shalom

Winner of the Jonathan Holden Poetry Chapbook Prize
2023
Choeofpleirn Press

THE TRUTH IS

Poems By

Vivienne Shalom

Winner of the Jonathan Holden
Poetry Chapbook Award

ISBN: (Digital) 979-8-9877852-9-4
        (Print) 979-8-9885631-0-5

Also available from Choeofpleirn Press
Linda Enders' *Consider the Gravity* (Finalist of the JH Poetry Chapbook Contest, 2023)
Amy Schumer's *Orbital Debris* (Winner of JH Poetry Chapbook Award, 2022)
Fran Schumer's *Weight* (Finalist of JH Poetry Chapbook Contest, 2022)

Choeofpleirn Press
Leavenworth, KS 66048
choeofpleirnpress@gmail.com
www.choeofpleirnpress.com

In Gratitude

Many thanks to my husband Stephen Soldz and son Isaac Soldz for their constant support, many readings and feedback on my poems, my brother Stephen Shalom for his technical assistance, my brother Jack Shalom for suggesting the final title, Connie Nelson for her careful reading, and most of all to Holly Guran for her comments on the manuscript and mentorship over the year. Finally, thank you to James P. Cooper and Ruth J. Heflin for being wonderful publishers to work with!

Dedication

For Sarina Shalom August 3rd, 1925—June 29th, 2021

Contents

How Do You Love?

Do you love like the turquoise sea
lapping the shore
til a mighty wave comes along
and blows you off course?

Do you love like the kayaker
on a hot summer's day
puddling through muddy waters
startled by a heron
fishing from shore.

Or do you love like a diver,
a leap from a slippery ledge
into crystal waters
fifty feet deep
to a quarry hidden from view?

Me, I love in great big gulps
greedy swallows
from one full glass.
I drink til every drop is gone
and even then
I drink some more.

The Beginning

I spent most of that trip to my mother's
in front of the computer
planning how to escape New York
before a lockdown.
Her eyes wanted to know
why I wasn't paying more attention to her.
I don't like the mask, she said.
I can't see you.
My brothers told me,
You better leave before it's too late.
When I arrived back in Boston
my family rushed me with hand sanitizer
and had me air out my suitcase.
It was March 2020.
This was only the beginning.

Coney Island Photograph

We are walking on the boardwalk
eating ice cream cones
heading to the Cyclone.

Our cousin shares stories
of England and the Beatles.
The ice cream is soft

melting quickly on this scorching day.
You show us how to lick around
the cone with your tongue

but the ice cream keeps dripping,
all over our hands and fingers.
You pass out napkins

from your handbag,
dab and wipe, even lick around
each of our cones.

The baby drops his on the ground
and wails, while mine starts to leak
through a hole on the bottom.

Drat! and *Bloody hell!* you cry
between fits of laughter.
You console the baby

with the rest of your cone,
send the oldest scrambling
for more napkins.

Wetting them with saliva
you wipe us clean.

Dustbusting

From her wheelchair throne
my mother is queen of the crumbs.
For years my siblings and I have joked
how no speck escapes her watchful eyes.
She tries to bend
but remembers she cannot
so just points to a spot of lint.
Quickly I run to grab the dustbuster.
No matter that my own dustbuster
lies on my kitchen table 500 miles away
uncharged for months.
I am what my friend Magda fondly calls
a "relaxed" housekeeper.
But now I bend because she cannot.
Fiercely, I suck up every bit of lint,
every stray thread, every last crumb
as if I were the daughter
she always wanted.

Visit

You are asleep at home
in the hospital bed,
a tiny bundle under covers.
I watch from the next bed
making sure you're still breathing.

You call out the name Renee,
your older sister who died years ago.
I know you mean me.
I go to you, take your hand
bruised from too many IV's.

I put my lips on your forehead
like you often did with me,
your skin soft at 94
a blue silk bonnet
still protecting your hairdo.

Our eyes meet, you smile
then drift back to sleep, mouth open.
I tiptoe back into bed remembering.
When dad was away on business trips
we kids took turns sleeping with you.

Though you complained about
us wriggling
I longed for my turn when you
wrapped your long legs around mine
and I inhaled your sweet breath.

Taking a Pass

Today I will take a pass
on the spate of sour-dough recipes,
the do-it-yourself masks,
the home-made hand sanitizer.

I will not read
"How to Shop Safely,"
"Where to Buy Toilet Paper,"
or "Seven Fruits and Veggies
that Stay Fresh for Months."

I will not watch
lockdown families dance,
handwashing demos,
or parading costumed cats.

I will not listen to
"Coronavirus Rhapsody,"
"Stayin Inside,"
or the COVID version of
"Sweet Caroline."

Tomorrow
I will rejoin the virtual army
of resilience
but today I will ditch my phone
and weep beneath a tree.

975 Ocean Parkway

She feels the cool breeze on her cheeks
as the caretaker wheels her
along Ocean Parkway.

The path is dotted with benches,
a Hassidic woman with a stroller,
two men playing chess.

Once this was called the Bridle Path.
She can't remember any horses
even back then.

She takes in the fragrance of roses,
marvels as cherry blossoms
fall like pink snow.

Soon the house will come into view.
For years she closed her eyes
each time she passed

the strange car in the driveway.
Now, it seems more like a story,
she wants retold—

a family around the table
songs and laughter
the clinking of glasses.

And the babies, the glorious babies
banging on pots on the kitchen floor,
while the mother stirs,

humming, *What a difference
a day makes…
Twenty-four little hours…*[*]

Her caretaker points,
So, Mrs. Shalom,
This was your house!

Yes, she nods,
for that's all she can manage.
Words are different now.

They don't make
sentences the way they used to.
Instead, they linger

in passageways,
veer off to distant rooms
and can't be called back.

* Written by Stanley Adams and Maria Grever, "What a
Difference a Day Makes" (1934).

Hand Washing

For now
I do not have to change the world
or anyone in it
including myself.
It is enough to look through the window
wonder about
the puffy white bird
with the grey and
black stripes
who sings for all of us.
It is enough to walk the nature trail
on rich green moss, held by the trees,
stirred by the leaves
unfurling.
It is enough to savor the blueberries
from today's gloved hands
Facetime my mother
love family and friends anew.
I do not have to emerge from this pandemic
with a debut bestseller
or even an organized pantry.
I'm finding a home in my own body
burrowing inside to a place
where it's enough just to "be"
where the social distance between us
was always an illusion.
I'm stepping off the production line
of my own making.
From now on
I wash my hands of it.

Facetime

My mother's caretaker
holds up the phone.
Can you see me? I ask.
Her face appears on my screen.
Depending on the day
a blank stare or a little nod.
Today a smile of recognition.

Her red stained lips
transport me to the perfumed hankies
she once used to blot her lipstick
folded in her handbag
along with the sticks of Juicy Fruit gum
and some crumpled receipts
she never could find.

I cannot feel her
but I know she is soft
because I melted into that warm flesh
thousands of times
though never enough times.

Do you know how beautiful you are? I say
You look very sweet, she says.

Sixty years of critiques
about my frizzy hair and ugly shoes
have been distilled into pure love.

No longer shy to sing aloud
we croon together across the miles:
Don't cry for me, Argentina...*
The truth is I never left you.

And we never did.
Leave each other, that is.
Only lost each other briefly
along the way.

* Written by Andrew Lloyd Weber and Rice Tim, "Don't
Cry for Me Argentina" (1976).

Mom, I Know You Wished
I Had Stayed in Brooklyn

You left England a war bride
to make America your home
How homesick you were.
Your mother wished you had stayed.

When I left for Boston at seventeen
I never admitted
how homesick I was,
to you or even myself.
Suffocated when I broke away
I first had to learn how to breathe.

Julio Iglesias

No use fighting for attention.
I've been replaced
by Julio Iglesias.
Since when was she even a fan?

My mother is swooning
to the song "Hey"
by nodding her head.

When her caretaker sings along
my mother's smile deepens.
Where is Julio taking her?

Can she understand the Spanish still?
Does she feel the passion,
the yearning for a perfect love?

Did my mother's dreams come true?
Did he live up to her
expectations?

Alone in my room
I play the English version.
I want not what is, but what could be.

I want one last connection
a moment that's ours
but she has already left with Julio.

Hard To Swallow

I.
Ochre leaves turning brown: November.
More than a year.
Still I focus on the inner landscape.

Pulling up to the library.
Never picking up my book on hold
because of a phone call from my brother:

Mom can't swallow anymore.
She aspirated twice already.
She will get her food

in the form of formula
through a tube
in her stomach.

II.
Those intimate lunches,
cheese sandwiches with tomato
we ate together from a tray

with Andrea Bocelli playing
in the background
after my father died.

In her glory, the huge festive
meals she made
with all of us around the table—

stuffed *meschi*, *yebra* with
melted apricots,
kibbe, *lahmajeen*, pickled cauliflower.

14

III.
I didn't think I could do it—
I was afraid I would measure wrong
or it would get plugged up

but we all learned.
It's amazing what you can
get used to.

But she never did.
In a family where food was the glue
that kept us together

she was alone.

Hair Wash Ritual

Every Friday night while the food is cooking
my mother brings the special pot
up to the bathroom
from under the kitchen sink.
No longer shiny, a dull silver,
used only for bath time.

She kneels by the tub,
stretching to reach the faucets
and run the water,
testing that it is just right
on her inner wrist.
I climb in, all legs, and let the water

surround me like the warm sea
my dark hair, thick with curls
cascading like a waterfall.
I don't know that her body aches
as she twists it by my side
her legs tucked under.

I have her all to myself
in this bathroom paradise
A cold squirt of shampoo, the smell of olives
as she gathers my hair into a lather
kneads my scalp like the dough
she uses for *sambousak*.

When she leans over to add fresh water,
it is never too hot so it would burn,
or too cold to make me shiver.
Her slender arms heave the pot up
and over me, a torrent of water,
pouring over my head and down my back

rinsing the soap to bathtub swirls.
Three potfuls, with my eyes squeezed tight
And a final potful
so the water flows
clear as chicken soup
and my hair shines blue-black.

She gathers me up
in the thickest green towel,
another one around my head

like a turban, and carries me off
to put on pajamas
for the Friday night meal.

Yellow

Walking along my old block in Brooklyn
none of the houses look the same.
That one, there, was gutted, garden mauled
the one I grew up in, bull-dozed
now an empty lot.

When our house was sold
my mother closed her eyes
every time we passed it.
It was the first time I understood
just what a house keeps inside.

But this is not about that
or the fact that I decided to get some fresh air
because my mother
may not make it this time,
that she is taken from me
piece by piece.

It is more about the tree
The one directly across the empty lot
whose blossoms are a new-born yellow
with petals as soft and as perfectly shaped
as a baby's toes,

a yellow so astonishing
that I pull out my phone to snap a photo.
This tree that had the audacity to bloom
on my old block in Brooklyn.

Ready

Six months in
drained from self-reflection
ready to emerge
not as a butterfly
but a very hungry caterpillar
ready to bite through that apple
lick off the frosting
binge on the banquet.

Ready to sweat off the sweatpants
slink into skin-tight sequined
spandex complete with fabulous face.
Yes! Uncork the champagne!
Strike up the bands!
Roll out the carpet!
Ready or not
here I come!

The Bowl from China

She never noticed the lotus flowers inside the bowl
or the stylized blue dragons that circled the outside
with curls of orange fire.
Her father brought it back from China
or the Orient as they called it.

The bowl sat on the table
when they curled up on the couch
to watch Jack Paar or listen to "My Fair Lady"
on the phonograph.
It sat there when her mother
put her feet up in those smelly satin slippers.

It stayed there as the children grew,
left home, returned with their own children
who bounced on grandma's lap.

She could have chosen anything
before the house was rummaged:
expensive jewelry, monogrammed cutlery.

But she wanted the bowl
This bowl that sat on the table
next to the couch in the den.

What Is Aleppo?

A question I could once answer
by way of my grandfather arriving
from Aleppo at Ellis Island—
he peddled women's collars

on the streets of New York—
and a grandmother who pinched
my cheeks and exclaimed, *Mashala!*
to express how I'd grown.

By way of the cumin, allspice, and cinnamon
that wafted through the kitchen
or the *yebra* with apricot, *meshi*
and *kibbe hamda.*

Now my story is part of rubble
the smell of death
the not so quiet desperation
of a man who flees with hardly time

to mourn his only child.
A child who wanted to play
outside with his truck,
when the bomb struck.

Bird Outside My Window

I've got the worst headache
and have to get out of here.
The puffy gray and white bird
has been chirping, no screeching
for three years.

I pick up the pieces I once called a life
and wipe them off with a dirty tissue.
Since the pandemic my nose
runs whenever I'm outside.

All those breaths I take
gasping for air
have been diagnosed as asthma.
There must be new insights
if I can find them in the pile of dirty
laundry or worn out sweats.

I want to connect with others
but I've lost all my social skills.
People seem cold and annoying.
I cross my arms in defensive mode.

The Woman Who Watched Time

In between whisking the kids off to school
and washing a load of laundry
the woman slipped off to the rose cushioned chair
her feet on the ottoman, eyes closed, lips pursed
and listened
listened for the glorious tick tock, tick tock, tick tock
that always started with the little dots
dots no bigger than an ellipsis
good little soldiers marching along
row after row.

Tick tock, tick tock, tick tock.
Slowly, one by one, each dot swelled
to the size of a full moon
their bellies pregnant with lush color
til finally they burst, spurting
and splattering their cardinal reds,
cobalt blues, canary yellows
onto the walls, the ceiling, the furniture
So that everything wet with paint
dripped with longing.

How to Turn Seventy

Drink a cup of coffee slowly
holding the mug with two weathered hands.
Step into the garden
no matter how small or imperfect.
Observe the beech tree dancing with the luminous sky.
Paint it in plein air
letting the bright yellows and greens stand out
against the muted background.
Paint the girl with the scraped knees
and Davy Crockett hat.
Splash on some cobalt blue for good luck.
Swing up to the sky on the garden swing
while the breeze brushes your cheek
and sun warms your shoulders.
Pick a song from your soundtrack
like "Me and Bobby McGee"
and sing it to the wind.
Name the people who have helped you grow and flourish,
laugh and play
while the others who never really got you
slip away.
Exclaim at the hummingbird
drinking nectar from the honeysuckle.
Freeze the moment.
Eat a sweet and juicy pear
and toss the pit
exactly where the future tree will grow.
Banish regrets to make room
For the precious moments left.
Witness how the dusk bathes the garden
in orange-pink-purple light.
Before dark
fall in love
with the whole damn planet.

Hospital Visit

I.
We called him "The Little Nazi"
the guard who blocked
passage to the rooms.
One visitor at a time
after a temperature check.
Short balding guy
raising his voice, his baton.
You'd think we were trying to crash
an exclusive nightclub.

II.
My mother did not have a death
like my father's.
His five children and wife
gathered around singing
the PS 99 school anthem,
extra folding chairs hauled in
for a steady stream
dropping by
all of us cheering when
Michael Phelps won a gold medal.

III.
I wait for my brother
to come down before I go up.
Did she eat? Is she talking?
We've gotten good at
quick summaries
which we know stress the positive
which we still want to hear.
This last year she barely talked.
I walk up to her hospital room
masked and yearning for contact.

IV.
She opens her eyes and smiles at me.
I try to explain the COVID system.
She turns her head.
I struggle to make conversation
but she is done for now.
I am not her most chatty child.
I long for my sister and brothers
to surround her together
that sense of family
that keeps us afloat.

Weary Traveler

Weary traveler at the doorstep
with your one-way ticket,
we've shared our goodbyes
and you've waved to us at the port.

#

The last time you crossed that ocean
was on the Queen Mary
returning to England
with a colicky baby girl

and a toddler boy who ran circles
all around the cabins.
One day clouds gathered
into a storm. You all took sick.

But soon you touched land, laden
with gifts for your mum and sisters
cashmeres, silk scarves, perfume,
chocolates from America.

Aah, the tears of joy, the stories
when you reached the other side.
You breathed *in* the Manchester air
and *out* the homesickness.

#

This time you are empty-handed
The dresses that turned heads
are hanging in the closet
soon to be given away.

27

The elegant blouses
are still in the drawers
petit and soft
smelling of your perfume.

This time you make the voyage alone
while we remain at shore
gathered like clouds
homesick without you.

Acknowledgments

"Dustbusting" and "Hand Washing" first appeared in *Tell-Tale Inklings #5.*

"FaceTime" was selected as part of "*The Mayor's Poetry Program 2023*" and displayed at City Hall.

About the Poet

Vivienne Shalom grew up in a large family in a tight-knit Syrian Jewish community in Brooklyn, New York. She has been a committee member of the Boston group "*Rozzie Reads Poetry*" for many years as well as a local featured poet. Two of her poems appeared in *Tell Tale Inkings #5*. Vivienne is the author of the children's book, *The Color of Things* (Rizzoli 1995). A former ESL teacher, graphic designer and welder, she is currently retired and active in her community and in the arts. She lives in Boston with her husband, Stephen Soldz.

These poems explore the journey of her mother's illness during the last years of her life. These years coincide with the covid 19 pandemic and bring up many memories.

Judge's Comments

The voice behind the collection of poems, *The Truth Is*, knows well the complicated relationships children have with their parents, especially the relationship daughters have with their mothers. In poems that span the years from being a child to being an adult, from the time her mother "carries me off/to put on pajamas," until the poet understands that her mother must "make the voyage alone/while we remain at shore," we are privileged to see how the poet taps into memory with fact and image, how she values both past and present, how, like the poet Yevtushenko, she shows us that "no life is uninteresting" and she, too, makes her "lament against destruction." For the poet's mother at the end of life, words "don't make/ sentences the way they used to/...and veer off into distant rooms." The words in these poems are precise, poignant, and poised between sadness and joy. They return us to our own distant rooms, allowing us a chance for exploration.

Anita Skeen, 2023 Judge
Author of *Never the Whole Story*; *The Resurrection of the Animals*;
Outside the Fold, Outside the Frame; and *Each Hand a Map*

Jonathan Holden Poetry Chapbook Contest

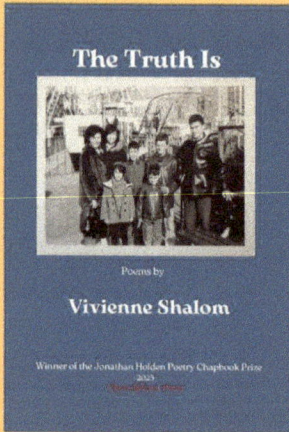

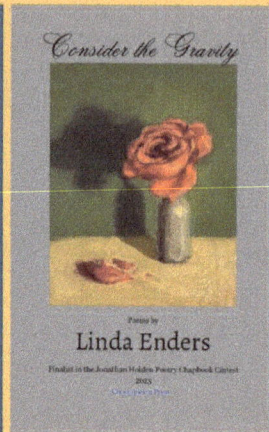

The Truth Is

Poems by

Vivienne Shalom

Winner of the Jonathan Holden Poetry Chapbook Prize
2023
Choeofpleirn Press

Consider the Gravity

Poems by

Linda Enders

Finalist in the Jonathan Holden Poetry Chapbook Contest
2023
Choeofpleirn Press

2023 Winner and Finalist

Choeofpleirn Press

Jonathan Holden Poetry Chapbook Contest

Sponsored by Choeofpleirn Press

Poets without a published chapbook or poetry book may enter.
Contest Fee: $20
Prize: 10 copies of printed chapbook and $250
See Submission Guidelines at
www.choeofpleirnpress.com/poetry-chapbook-contest
for details.

Thank you for supporting our press!

Fun Fact

Choeofpleirn

pronounced "chuf-plern"

is a combination of our
surnames by alternating
the letters

www.choeofpleirnpress.com

Choeofpleirn Press
www.choeofpleirnpress.com
choeofpleirnpress@gmail.com

www.ingramcontent.com/pod-product-compliance
Lightning Source LLC
Chambersburg PA
CBHW052026030426
42335CB00026B/3303